AF882113

Manifesting Bot

Use ChatGPT to Create the Life You Want

ChatGPT & the Law of Attraction

Manifest Love, Money & Happiness with Your AI Partner

Sugar Gay Isber McMillan

The WOW Book Co.™
Austin, Texas

Manifesting Bot: Use ChatGPT to Create the Life You Want

© 2025 Sugar Gay Isber McMillan. All rights reserved.

No part of this publication may be reproduced, stored in a retrieval system, or transmitted in any form or by any means—electronic, mechanical, photocopying, recording, or otherwise, without prior written permission of the publisher, except in the case of brief quotations used in reviews or articles.

This book is published for educational and personal reference. The author and publisher disclaim responsibility for any liability, loss, or risk, personal or otherwise, incurred as a direct or indirect consequence of the use and application of the contents of this book.

Published by **The WOW Book Co.™**
Austin, Texas, USA

ISBN: 978-1-967973-51-4

Book design by The WOW Book Co.™
Logo and QR codes included with permission.

Large-Print Edition

Printed in the United States of America

Dedication

For everyone.
Because manifesting isn't for the few, it's for all of us.
May this book remind you that clarity, hope and joy are already within your reach.

Xx, Sugar Gay Isber McMillan

Epigraph

"Go confidently in the direction of your dreams.
Live the life you have imagined."
— Henry David Thoreau

Table of Contents

Introduction

I still remember the first time my son handed me a book on manifesting. It was *Asking It Is Given*, and I carried it around like it was my Bible. I read and reread it. I bent the corners of the pages. I wrote myself a check and tucked it into my wallet. I did everything it told me to do.

Later, I went to one of the live events here in Austin. In that room, I was told something I'll never forget: *You're in the vortex.* And I knew I was.

How did I know? Because things lined up for me:

- I always seemed to find the perfect parking space.
- When I think of someone, they often call me.
- When I needed money, it came.
- My long-term goals started showing up faster than I thought possible.

That was my first taste of the **power of words and deliberate intention.** When I got clear and added emotion, my energy shifted. I began to realize how much control we actually have over what we attract.

This book explores the application of that practice in today's world. We spend a significant amount of time on our computers and phones. Why not make them part of the process? Why not train your chatbot to be your helper in manifesting?

Your chatbot can be trained to help you:

- Rewrite vague wishes into clear, powerful goals.
- Create affirmations and visualization scripts.
- Break big dreams into small, doable steps.
- Remind you daily of what matters most.

Manifesting is not magic. It is clarity plus focus plus consistency. With your chatbot by your side, you can keep practicing even when life gets hectic.

This is the modern way. This is today's way. And it works.

Let's begin.

Chapter 1. The Power of Words & Deliberate Intention

When I was five years old, I discovered my mother's old Pollyanna books. They were printed decades earlier, but I read them like they were brand new treasures. Pollyanna was an orphan who believed in her father's "glad game," the practice of finding something to be glad about in every situation. Her joy and optimism changed her aunt, her neighbors, and her entire town.

I devoured every book. My dad even asked the library to order the ones I didn't have. From that young age, I knew: everything works out somehow. That belief became my first understanding of manifesting.

Words, the words we think, speak, and repeat, carry power. They shape our perspective and what we attract.

Ancient Roots of the Power of Words

- In India, mantras have been repeated for centuries to align the mind and spirit.
- In Egypt and Greece, Hermetic teachings gave us the phrase: *"As above, so below."* The belief was that your inner world reflects your outer world.

- In Stoic philosophy, words were used to frame hardships as opportunities for growth.

The idea that words shape life is as old as humanity itself.

The Modern History of Manifesting Words

- Dale Carnegie (1936): His *How to Win Friends and Influence People* showed how words, influence, and deliberate thought could build success. Carnegie studied leaders and proved that optimism and positive influence could change lives.
- Napoleon Hill (1937): In *Think and Grow Rich*, Hill laid out the connection between affirmations, persistence, and achievement. His turning point came from industrialist Andrew Carnegie, who urged him to study successful people and discover their "secrets." Hill called it the "definite chief aim", writing your goal in clear words and repeating it daily.
- Andrew Carnegie himself once said:

"I took possession of my own mind, and that mind has yielded me every material thing I want, and much more than I need."

- Earl Nightingale (1956): His famous audio recording *The Strangest Secret* summarized it simply:

"We become what we think about."

Generations of teachers, from mystics to CEOs, all return to the same truth: your words direct your life.

Why Words Matter in Manifesting

- Vague wishes create vague results.
- Clear words focus your energy and attention.
- When you repeat words with emotion, you train your subconscious to expect the result.

Quick Practice

1. Write down a vague dream: *I want to be happier.*
2. Ask your bot: *“Rewrite this dream as a clear, positive goal.”*
3. Compare the difference:
   - Vague: *I want to be happier.*
   - Clear: *I choose joy every day by noticing what is good in my life and adding one new activity each week that excites me.*

That’s the power of words.

Key Idea

Your words are not just sounds. They are instructions to your brain and signals to the universe. Use them with clarity and intention, and they will shape your world.

Chapter 2. Affirmations Made Easy

Affirmations are statements of belief repeated with purpose. They retrain your mind, lift your mood, and align your energy with what you want to attract.

My First Taste of Affirmations

Reading the Pollyanna books as a child planted the seed, but my adult practice deepened when my son gave me a book on manifesting. I carried it everywhere, highlighted it, folded its corners, and tried every exercise.

One simple practice, repeating positive statements daily, felt almost too easy at first. But I noticed that when I said something long enough, I began to believe it. And when I believed it, things began to shift.

A History of Affirmations

Ancient mantras aligned thoughts with divine order.

New Thought authors like Wallace Wattles (*The Science of Getting Rich*) taught that affirmations train your subconscious.

Napoleon Hill instructed readers to repeat their "definite chief aim" daily until it became reality.

Earl Nightingale declared: *"We become what we think about."* His affirmation-based teachings are still quoted today.

Even Oprah Winfrey has shared that affirmations and gratitude journaling shaped her path, saying: *"You don't become what you want, you become what you believe."*

Why Affirmations Work

They shift your attention from fear to possibility.

They reprogram your subconscious.

They build momentum through repetition.

How to Use Your Bot for Affirmations

Your chatbot can help you create affirmations that feel natural and believable:

"Write 10 affirmations for self-confidence that sound encouraging but not fake."

"Create daily affirmations for money and abundance that I can use in the morning."

"Help me turn this fear into a positive affirmation: I'm always behind at work."

Practice

Write a fear: *I'll never get ahead financially.*

Ask your bot to flip it.

Result: *"I am learning how to manage my money and create new streams of income."*

Repeat daily with emotion.

Key Idea

Affirmations are not magic words. They are daily reminders that align your mind and energy. With your bot, you can refresh them anytime, making the practice easy and powerful.

Chapter 3. Visualization Scripts

Affirmations shape what you say. Visualization shapes what you see and feel. Together, they create a powerful manifesting practice.

Why Visualization Works

The brain does not fully distinguish between real and imagined events.

Athletes use visualization to rehearse every movement of a game or race.

Neuroscience shows that visualization activates the same neural pathways as real action.

When you visualize with emotion, you practice success in advance.

Words + Pictures

Words give structure.

Pictures give emotion and detail.

Together, they make your dream feel inevitable.

Using Your Bot for Visualization Scripts

Your chatbot can generate guided meditations or visualization exercises:

"Write a 5-minute visualization where I walk through my dream home."

"Help me imagine my ideal workday from start to finish."

"Create a script where I visualize giving a speech and receiving applause."

Practice

Choose a dream: *Publishing my book.*

Ask your bot to write a visualization.

Read it slowly, eyes closed.

Add emotion, pride, joy, relief.

Repeat daily.

Add Your Senses

Visualization without senses is like a movie on mute. Turn the sound on:

Hear the music at your celebration.

Smell the fresh paint in your dream home.

Taste the champagne of success.

Feel the sun on your face during your vacation.

Real-World Examples

Olympic athletes visualize their races daily before competing.

Public speakers imagine the applause before they walk on stage.

Entrepreneurs picture signing contracts before deals close.

These practices aren't "woo-woo." They're mainstream tools of performance and success.

Key Idea

Visualization makes the unseen seen. With your bot as your scriptwriter, you can practice your dream until your body and mind accept it as reality. And once you do, your life begins to line up with the vision.

Creativity is not a gift for the few –

It's a channel open to everyone

Chapter 4. Gratitude and Journaling

Gratitude is not just about saying "thanks." It is about shifting your entire outlook. It is one of the most powerful forces in manifesting because it changes how you feel in the moment and how you see the world tomorrow.

Journaling is the partner that makes gratitude practical. When you take a thought and put it on paper, you lock it into your mind and body. Gratitude lifts your energy. Journaling grounds it. Together, they create a practice that accelerates manifesting.

The Science of Gratitude

For decades, psychologists and neuroscientists have been studying gratitude. The results are striking:

- Researchers at the University of California, Davis, found that people who kept gratitude journals exercised more, slept better, and felt more optimistic about the week ahead.
- A study of college students showed that gratitude practices reduced stress and boosted resilience during exams.

- Another study with veterans found that writing gratitude letters lowered symptoms of depression and post-traumatic stress.

- Brain scans show that gratitude activates the **prefrontal cortex**, the part of the brain tied to focus, planning, and positive emotion. It also lowers cortisol, the stress hormone, which means your body physically relaxes when your mind turns toward gratitude.

In other words, gratitude is not just an emotional response; it is a biological one.

Real-World Examples

- **Oprah Winfrey** has been keeping a gratitude journal for decades. She credits this daily habit as one of the biggest reasons for her success. She once said: *"If you look at what you have in life, you'll always have more. If you look at what you don't have, you'll never have enough."* Her simple practice was to write down five things she was grateful for each day. It changed the way she approached every challenge.

- **Soldiers in recovery programs** have used gratitude journaling to heal from trauma. Writing about the small wins, a good night's sleep, a letter from home, a kind word from a fellow soldier, gave them the resilience to keep going.

- **Students under pressure** often use gratitude practices to manage anxiety. Taking just three minutes to write about what went well that day shifts their mindset from panic to possibility. Teachers who introduced gratitude journals in classrooms noticed calmer students and better focus.

Gratitude is not abstract. It shows up in real lives, real healing, real results.

Why Gratitude Accelerates Manifesting

Manifesting works when you align your energy with abundance. Gratitude does this in two ways:

1. It shifts your focus from what's missing to what's already here.
2. It raises your emotional vibration so new opportunities flow in more easily.

Think of your brain like a search engine. When you say, *"I'm grateful for this,"* you're typing in a keyword. Your brain starts searching for more of it. That's why when you buy a red car, you suddenly see red cars everywhere. Gratitude trains your mind to notice abundance.

When you practice gratitude, you stay in the vortex. You keep your attention on what is working, and that pulls in more of it.

Journaling: Writing Your Way Into Alignment

Journaling gives structure to gratitude. It is where you:

- Release negative thoughts by unloading them onto paper.
- Spot patterns in your beliefs and habits.
- Track progress and see how far you've come.
- Strengthen your trust in yourself by recording your intentions.

Even five minutes a day is enough to change how you feel. The act of writing is like giving your subconscious a blueprint.

The 3-3-3 Rule

For individuals new to manifesting or those who feel stuck, the **3-3-3 rule** is a powerful tool. Here's how it works:

- Write down a specific desire or goal as an affirmative statement 33 times a day for 3 consecutive days.
- Example: *"I am grateful that I now earn $5,000 a month doing work I love."*
- The process aligns your thoughts and vibrations with your goal.
- It programs your subconscious to treat this desire as real, familiar, and possible.

Why it works: repetition creates belief. And belief creates momentum.

Words Have Consequences

I tell my husband this often: your words are not just sounds, they are instructions to your brain. Every time you think or say something negative, you are teaching your mind to look for more of it.

- Say "I'm tired" all day, and your body responds with more fatigue.
- Say "I never get a break," and your mind filters out the opportunities you do have.
- Flip those same words into gratitude, "I'm grateful for the rest I get," or "I'm glad I have work to do", and your brain shifts.

Your words have power inside your body. They shape your energy, your biology, and your future. Gratitude helps you use that power wisely.

Using Your Bot for Gratitude and Journaling

Your chatbot can make this practice easier and more fun. It can:

- Generate fresh gratitude prompts every day.

- Reframe complaints into grateful statements.
- Create journaling exercises that help you dig deeper.
- Remind you to keep going when life gets busy.

Sample Prompts

- *"Give me 10 gratitude prompts that focus on health."*
- *"Write three journaling questions about what went well today."*
- *"Help me turn this complaint into gratitude: I hate my job."*

Practices to Try

1. The Daily Gratitude List

Each morning, write down three things you are grateful for. Keep them simple. Example: *My morning coffee. My healthy body. My supportive friend.*

2. The Evening Journaling Check-In

At night, answer two questions:

- *What went well today?*
- *What do I want to release before sleep?*

3. The Gratitude Letter

Once a week, write a short note to someone you appreciate. You don't even need to send it. The act of writing builds joy.

4. The Bot Boost

Ask your bot to keep you accountable:

- *"Ask me every night at 9pm to write three things I'm grateful for."*
- *"Remind me weekly to write a gratitude letter."*

5. The 3-3-3 Practice

Pick one desire. Write it as an affirmation. Repeat it 33 times for 3 days. Example: *"I am grateful for my healthy, strong body."* Watch how your energy begins to shift.

Gratitude in Mainstream Culture

Gratitude has moved from philosophy to the mainstream.

- **Oprah's daily journal** is legendary. Millions of people followed her lead.
- **CEOs** use gratitude journaling to keep perspective under stress.
- **Athletes** visualize success and keep gratitude rituals to sharpen focus.
-

- **Schools** are adding gratitude practices into classrooms to build resilience in students.
- **Therapists** use gratitude journaling as a tool to treat depression and anxiety.

Gratitude has become a universal practice because it works.

Key Idea

Gratitude is the fuel. Journaling is the vehicle. And your bot is the co-pilot that keeps you moving. Together, they don't just make you feel better in the moment, they accelerate manifesting by shifting your words, your focus, and your energy toward the life you want.

A dream without action

Is a seed left in the packet.

Chapter 5. From Dream to Action

Dreams are beautiful. They're the spark that lights your imagination and the compass that points you forward. But a dream without action is like a seed left in the packet, full of potential, but never blossoming.

Manifesting is not about sitting still and waiting. It's about believing, aligning, and **acting with intention**. This chapter shows how to bridge the gap between vision and reality, with the help of your chatbot.

Faith without action is wishful thinking.

Action without faith is just work. Together, they create flow.

Why Action Matters

Napoleon Hill wrote in *Think and Grow Rich* that "A goal is a dream with a deadline." Without action, dreams remain abstract. Action gives them form.

- **Faith + Action = Results.** Faith alone is wishful thinking. Action alone is hard work without alignment. Together, they create flow.

- **Tiny Steps Compound.** Small actions daily beat giant leaps once a year.
- **Momentum Feeds Belief.** When you take a step, you see progress, which strengthens faith, which makes the next step easier.

The Science of Small Wins

Psychologists call it the **progress principle**: people are happiest and most motivated when they see small wins. Even a minor step toward your dream rewires your brain for persistence.

- Teresa Amabile, Harvard researcher, found that tracking small daily progress boosted motivation more than big achievements.
- That means writing 200 words of your novel today is as powerful for your brain as finishing the whole book.

Tiny steps daily beat giant leaps once a year.

How to Move from Dream to Action

Step 1. Clarify the Dream

Vague: "I want to write a book."
Clear: "I want to write a 50,000-word memoir draft by next December."

Prompt to Try: "Help me rewrite my dream as a specific, measurable goal."

Step 2. Break It Down

Big goals overwhelm. Breaking them into smaller milestones makes them manageable.

- Draft an outline.
- Write one chapter a week.
- Celebrate each finished page.

Prompt to Try: "Create a step-by-step plan for writing my first book, broken down by months and weeks."

Step 3. Schedule It

If it's not scheduled, it's a wish. Use your bot to create a realistic timeline.

Prompt to Try: "Help me design a weekly schedule where I spend 30 minutes daily on my dream."

Step 4. Balance Faith with Flexibility

Act boldly, but don't strangle the process. If something doesn't work, adjust. Faith means trusting that even detours move you closer.

Momentum is built on small wins, stack enough of them, and your dream becomes inevitable

---

Real-World Examples

- **Walt Disney** dreamed of Disneyland when most thought it was impossible. He started with sketches, then a small model, then pitches. Every step brought the dream closer until millions could walk inside it.
- **Sara Blakely**, founder of Spanx, wrote down her dream of creating footless pantyhose. She chipped away at it after work hours, made calls, and took small actions until the product hit shelves. Today she's a billionaire, all because she broke a dream into steps.
- **Oprah Winfrey** often says: "You get in life what you have the courage to ask for." She didn't stop at dreaming about success, she took every opportunity, prepared relentlessly, and let aligned action turn vision into reality.

Bot-Powered Action Planning

Your bot can't walk the path for you, but it can light the way.

Here's how your bot can turn dreams into plans:

- **Weekly Check-Ins:** *"Ask me every Sunday what I accomplished toward my goal and help me plan the next step."*
- **Accountability Partner:** *"Pretend you are my coach. Ask me three tough questions about whether I stayed on track this week."*
- **Obstacle Solver:** *"List three possible solutions if I don't have money to fund my project."*
- **Energy Manager:** *"Help me design a routine that leaves space for rest and creativity while I pursue my goal."*

Balancing Action with Flow

Manifesting isn't grinding. It's aligned action. When you're forcing every step with tension, you're out of sync. But when you take inspired action, steps that feel purposeful, even joyful, you stay in flow.

Think of it like rowing with the current instead of against it. You're still working, but the water carries you further with less effort.

My Nightly Ritual: Turning Dreams into Tomorrow's Actions

For me, manifesting isn't just something I do in the morning with a journal or a checklist. It's also what I do every night before I fall asleep. It has become one of the most powerful practices of my life.

Here's how it works:

I lay flat on my back, straight and still, so my body feels aligned. I close my eyes and on the inside of my eyelids, I see a horizon stretching out before me. That horizon becomes my canvas. While I focus on that steady line, I begin with gratitude. I replay my day, every small win, every good moment, every reason I can say, *I'm glad I had this day.*

From gratitude, I shift into intention. I imagine what I want tomorrow to look like. I see myself moving through my day with clarity and ease. I outline in my mind the specific results I want to create, sometimes it's a conversation, sometimes it's progress on a project, sometimes it's the feeling of lightness I want to carry. I hold that vision gently, almost like a dream I'm planting into the night.

And then, as I drift, my subconscious takes over. My dreams are vivid, sometimes wild and colorful, filled with singing and dancing, sometimes practical and surprising, offering ideas for my jewelry designs or flashes of inspiration for the books I'm working on. I see potentials opening, goals blossoming, creative sparks catching fire.

This ritual keeps me from ever feeling that sleep is wasted time. My nights are as active as my days, only in a different dimension. When I wake, I carry pieces of those dreams with me, translating them into actions, designs, conversations, and next steps.

This is what "from dream to action" means to me: ending each day with gratitude, aligning with intention, and letting both my waking mind and my dreaming self move me closer to what I want.

- **"Schedule your dream. If it's not on your calendar, it's just a wish."**
- **"Tiny steps daily beat giant leaps once a year."**
- **"Faith + Action = Results."**
- **"Your bot can't walk the path for you, but it can light the way."**

Key Practices

1. **Dream Mapping**
   Write your dream. Ask your bot to expand it into a clear plan.

2. **The Rule of One Step**
   Every day, do one small thing toward your goal. Send an email, write a page, research one resource.
3. **Bot as Project Manager**
   Let your bot track tasks, deadlines, and wins.
4. **Celebrate Micro Wins**
   Thank yourself for progress. Thank your bot for support. Gratitude accelerates the cycle.

The Bottom Line

Dreams don't manifest in one giant leap. They unfold step by step. Your faith fuels your vision, your action shapes it, and your bot helps you organize it all.

Remember: clarity sparks intention, gratitude fuels momentum, and **action is the bridge** that turns thought into reality.

"Every action you take teaches your subconscious that your dream is real."

Take a few minutes to practice. Use this space to connect your dream to action.

1. My Dream (in one clear sentence):

____

2. Three Small Steps I Can Take This Week:

- ________________________
- ________________________
- ________________________

3. Affirmation for Today:

____

4. One Bot Prompt I Will Try Tonight:

____

____

____

Chapter 6. Manifesting for Specifics

When people first hear about manifesting, their minds often jump straight to the “big four”: **love, money, health, and creativity**. These are the areas where we long for transformation, and where clear, consistent manifesting practices can make a profound difference.

What makes manifesting powerful is not that it “magically delivers” your desires overnight, but that it sharpens your focus, lifts your energy, and aligns you with the opportunities already around you. When you pair that focus with belief and action, incredible things can happen.

Your bot can be your mirror, your coach and your cheerleader in every area of life.

Love and Relationships

Love is universal, everyone wants to give it, and everyone wants to receive it. Yet so often, people settle for less than they deserve because they haven’t taken the time to clarify what they want.

The Partner Checklist

One of the most effective exercises in manifesting love is the **checklist method**. Write out in detail the qualities you want in a partner. Not vague words like "nice" or "fun," but deeply specific desires:

- Loves family but respects independence.
- Laughs easily and has a playful spirit.
- Enjoys traveling and exploring new foods.
- Is financially responsible and generous.
- Shares values of kindness, honesty, and growth.

When you write this out and revisit it often, something fascinating happens: you begin to notice these qualities in people you meet. You stop wasting energy on relationships that don't match your values.

Write your partner checklist and then release it. The universe can only deliver what you've defined."

Prompt to Try: "Help me create a detailed partner checklist in positive language."

Real-World Examples

- **Elizabeth Gilbert**, author of *Eat, Pray, Love*, famously wrote about how clarifying what she wanted in relationships completely shifted the people she attracted into her life.
- Countless readers of Esther Hicks' *Ask and It Is Given* have reported meeting their partners after doing similar exercises.

The point isn't that the universe drops a person at your doorstep, it's that by writing and affirming, you begin to *expect love* instead of doubt it, and that expectation changes everything.

You become what you rehearse, in your words,

your visions, and your actions.

Money and Career

For many, money is the loudest need. But money isn't just about numbers in a bank account, it's about energy, security, and freedom.

From Scarcity to Abundance

When you see money as scarce, you cling. When you see it as abundant, you flow. Zig Ziglar put it bluntly: "Positive thinking will let you do everything better than negative thinking will."

Earl Nightingale, in *The Strangest Secret*, declared: *"We become what we think about."* If you think constantly about debt and lack, that's where your energy stays. If you think about opportunity and possibility, you begin to notice ways to grow.

Case Study: Jim Carrey's $10 Million Check

In the 1990s, actor Jim Carrey was a struggling comedian. He wrote himself a check for $10 million for "acting services rendered," dated five years in the future. He carried it in his wallet, visualized success daily, and worked tirelessly toward his dream. By 1994, he had landed *Dumb and Dumber* and received, you guessed it, a paycheck for $10 million.

That's the power of clarity, belief, and persistence.

Prompt to Try: "Help me design a 12-month money map that includes savings, debt payoff, and side income ideas."

Career Applications

Your bot can help with:

- Mock interviews.
- Drafting resumes or LinkedIn updates.
- Exploring side hustles that match your interests.
- Creating daily affirmations about financial success.

When paired with manifesting practices, these actions accelerate your progress.

Health and Wellness

Health is the foundation of everything. Without it, money, love, and creativity lose their shine.

Manifesting health doesn't mean ignoring doctors or pretending illness isn't real. It means aligning your inner focus with vitality and healing, so your choices naturally move toward well-being.

Examples

- **Louise Hay**, author of *You Can Heal Your Life*, taught millions that words and thoughts can shape physical health.
- Modern research confirms that stress, negativity, and hopelessness can weaken immunity, while gratitude, joy, and optimism strengthen it.

Bot-Powered Health

- Ask your bot for 5-minute energy routines.
- Create meal plans that emphasize vitality.
- Generate health affirmations like: *"I honor my body by feeding it well and resting it deeply."*

Prompt to Try: "Write me a morning routine that boosts energy and sets a positive tone."

Creativity and Flow

Creativity isn't reserved for artists. It's in problem-solving, parenting, cooking, even reorganizing your closet. Manifesting creativity is about opening the channel and trusting the flow.

Famous Examples

- **Eckhart Tolle** teaches presence as the gateway to inspiration. When you're in the "now," ideas come easier.
- **Julia Cameron's** *The Artist's Way* is filled with affirmations and exercises that mirror manifesting practices, morning pages, affirmations, and affirming creative recovery.

Bot-Powered Creativity

- Ask your bot for a daily creative challenge.
- Let it generate prompts for painting, writing, or brainstorming.
- Record a visualization of yourself finishing your project, then listen back for motivation.

Expanding Your World Through Teachers

Manifesting has a long lineage. Here are voices worth knowing:

- **Napoleon Hill**, *Think and Grow Rich*, built on interviews with Andrew Carnegie.
- **Dale Carnegie**, *How to Win Friends and Influence People*, showing how influence begins with inner mindset.
- **Eckhart Tolle**, presence as power.
- **Zig Ziglar**, attitude as altitude.

- **Esther Hicks**, the vortex, alignment with joy.

Don't know where to begin? Ask your bot.

Prompt to Try: "Give me a short guide to the teachings of Napoleon Hill and how they connect to manifesting."

Practical Techniques

1. **The Partner Checklist**, Write it, refine it, then let it go.
2. **The Money Map**, Ask your bot to create a yearlong financial plan.
3. **The Health 3-3-3 Rule**, Write one positive statement 33 times daily for three days. Example: *"I am strong, healthy, and thriving."*
4. **Creative Spark Journal**, Ask your bot for one daily prompt and record your results.

Gratitude is a magnet. Action is a bridge

The Bottom Line

Manifesting specifics isn't about luck. It's about clarity, focus, and aligning your energy with your goals. Jim Carrey's check, Oprah's gratitude journals, Zig Ziglar's attitude, Tolle's presence, these aren't accidents. They're examples of people living in alignment with their vision.

You can do the same. And now, with a chatbot as your daily partner, you don't have to remember all the steps, you can simply ask, and the guidance is right there, 24/7.

This is where you apply manifesting to the specifics that matter most to you.

1. My Partner Checklist (top 5 qualities):

- ______________________________
- ______________________________
- ______________________________
- ______________________________
- ______________________________

2. My Money Goal for the Next Year:

____

3. One Health Affirmation I Will Use Daily:

____

4. A Creative Prompt to Try Today:

____

5. A Mentor I Will Learn From (book, podcast, or quote):

Try This Prompt (Love):
"Help me create a detailed partner checklist in positive, present-tense language."

Try This Prompt (Money):
"Design a 12-month financial plan that includes savings, debt payoff, and new income streams."

Try This Prompt (Health):
"Write me a morning routine that boosts energy and sets a positive tone for the day."

Try This Prompt (Creativity):
"Give me a daily creative challenge I can do in under 10 minutes."

Try This Prompt (Mentors):
"Summarize the teachings of Eckhart Tolle, Napoleon Hill, or Zig Ziglar and show me how to apply them this week."

Or even just this:

"Help me design a weekly schedule where I spend 30 minutes daily on my dream."

Chapter 7. Removing Blocks

Manifesting doesn't fail because dreams are too big. It fails because blocks get in the way. These blocks aren't out there in the world. They live inside us, in our beliefs, our patterns, and the stories we tell ourselves.

The good news is that every block can be softened, questioned, and rewritten. And your bot can be a partner in helping you see what you can't always see for yourself.

What Are Blocks?

Blocks are the inner "no's" that cancel out your outer "yes."

- You say you want love, but you secretly believe you're not lovable.
- You want wealth, but you grew up hearing that "money is the root of all evil."
- You dream of health, but deep down you've convinced yourself that illness runs in your family, so it's inevitable.

Blocks aren't truths. They're *scripts.* And scripts can be rewritten.

"Blocks are not walls. They are scripts. And scripts can be rewritten."

How to Spot a Block

The first step is noticing. Most of us carry limiting beliefs without ever questioning them.

Ask yourself:

- What patterns keep repeating in my life?
- What excuses do I return to again and again?
- What stories do I tell myself when I fail or get stuck?

These are the fingerprints of a block.

"The words you whisper to yourself are the architecture of your future."

Reframing Limiting Beliefs

Psychologists call it **cognitive reframing**. It means taking a thought and turning it inside out until you see it in a new way.

Example:

- Block: "I can't manage money."

- Reframe: “I am learning how to manage money with more skill every day.”

Example:

- Block: “I always attract the wrong partners.”
- Reframe: “I am becoming clearer about what I want, and I now attract people who align with me.”

Reframing doesn’t deny reality. It resets it.

Try This Prompt:
“Help me reframe the belief ‘I always fail at dieting’ into a positive statement that feels true but also stretches me.”

Shadow Work

The term “shadow” comes from Carl Jung. It describes the hidden parts of ourselves we’d rather not face. Fear, shame, guilt, anger, the things we push down.

But here’s the truth: what you push down leaks out anyway. Shadow work is about shining a gentle light.

Practical shadow prompts:

- “Why does this trigger me?”
- “What am I afraid of people seeing in me?”
- “What would it feel like if I forgave myself for this?”

Your bot can help here, too. You can ask it to role-play as a compassionate guide, asking gentle questions that open doors.

"Your shadow is not your enemy. It is your unclaimed teacher."

Real-World Examples of Block Breaking

- **Oprah Winfrey** grew up hearing she wasn't enough, poor, overlooked, and dismissed. She reframed that story and became one of the most influential voices in the world.
- **J.K. Rowling** faced rejection after rejection for *Harry Potter.* If she had let "I'm a failure" win, millions of readers would have been deprived of a magical world.
- **Tony Robbins** teaches that "where focus goes, energy flows." He's built an empire by helping people reframe their beliefs about possibility.

Each of these people didn't just dream, they broke through blocks.

Try This Prompt:

"Act as my life coach. Ask me five questions to uncover the beliefs holding me back from success."

Flipping "I Can't" Into "I Am Becoming"

One of the simplest and most powerful practices is swapping "I can't" for "I am becoming."

- "I can't save money" → "I am becoming someone who saves money with ease."
- "I can't stay healthy" → "I am becoming stronger and healthier every day."
- "I can't finish big projects" → "I am becoming consistent in finishing what I start."

This gentle shift opens the door for growth.

"I can't" ends the sentence. I am becoming' begins the journey."

Using Your Bot as a Mirror

Sometimes you can't hear your own limiting belief until you say it out loud, or write it. That's where your bot comes in.

Ask it:

- "Rewrite this negative thought in a way that empowers me."
- "Show me three positive reframes for the belief that I'll never find love."
- "Help me create a mantra that replaces my self-doubt."

Try This Prompt:
"Take this thought, 'I'm too old to start over', and show me three affirmations that prove the opposite."

The Practice of Compassion

Breaking blocks isn't about shaming yourself. It's about compassion. When you meet your block with love instead of judgment, it loosens its grip.

Say to yourself: *I'm learning. I'm growing. I'm rewriting my story.*

"Compassion is the solvent that dissolves blocks."

Your Turn

Take 10 minutes to work through the exercises below. Be honest. Let your answers surprise you.

1. A Block I Keep Bumping Into:

---

2. The Story I Tell Myself About It:

---

3. A Reframe That Opens a New Door:

---

4. My "I Am Becoming" Statement:

---

5. A Bot Prompt I Will Use to Explore This Block:

The Bottom Line

Blocks aren't barriers. They're teachers. Every limiting belief is an invitation to step into a new story. By using gratitude, reframing, shadow work, and your bot's gentle guidance, you can turn your inner "no" into an empowered "yes."

When you learn to recognize your blocks, you stop being trapped by them. And when you stop being trapped, your dreams are free to move forward, step by step, becoming real.

Chapter 8. Seasonal and Holiday Manifesting

Manifesting doesn't only happen in the quiet, everyday moments. It also thrives in the rhythms of time, the turning of the year, the cycle of the moon, the special days that hold meaning. These are natural markers, invitations to reset and realign.

Holidays, birthdays, and seasonal shifts remind us that time is not just passing, it's presenting us with fresh opportunities. When you learn to use these natural cycles to strengthen your focus, your manifesting power expands.

New Year Intentions

The new year has always been a sacred moment for intention. Cultures all over the world create rituals of release and renewal: resolutions, prayers, feasts, fasts.

But here's the shift: Instead of vague resolutions that fade by February, you can use your bot to create *clarity and structure.*

- Prompt it to write a New Year Manifesto with you.
- Ask it to design a 12-month roadmap broken into clear, achievable steps.
- Use it to remind you monthly to check in on your progress.

"The new year is not just a date. It's a doorway."

Lunar Cycles and Full Moon Rituals

Ancient traditions honored the moon as a marker of energy and timing. The new moon is for planting seeds. The full moon is for harvest, reflection, and release.

You can harness this by asking your bot to guide you through lunar rituals:

- Write out what you want to release under a full moon.
- Journal your intentions at the new moon.
- Create affirmations tied to lunar phases.

Try This Prompt:

"Write me a guided script for a full moon release ritual, focusing on letting go of old fears and opening to new opportunities."

Birthdays as Personal New Years

Your birthday is your personal reset button. It's a natural moment for reflection and redirection.

- Ask your bot: "Help me design a birthday ritual to celebrate who I've become and clarify what's next."
- Use your birthday to write a new story about yourself, the year ahead as a chapter in your life's book.

"Your birthday isn't just a reminder of age. It's a reminder of power."

Holiday Resets

The holidays can stir stress and joy in equal measure. They remind us of tradition but also sometimes trigger old wounds. That makes them powerful manifesting moments.

You can reset by:

- Writing gratitude letters instead of only buying gifts.
- Asking your bot for calm scripts when family tensions rise.
- Creating affirmations for generosity, patience, and joy.

Try This Prompt:
"Give me three affirmations for staying calm and grounded during holiday gatherings."

The Big Two: Health and Wealth

Seasonal manifesting isn't only about dates on the calendar. It's about aligning with the two areas most people struggle with: **money and health.**

When you're worried about bills or your body, you vibrate scarcity. The Law of Attraction responds not to what you *say* you want but to what you *feel* is true.

- **Money**: Start telling a new money story. Ask your bot to help you write affirmations that shift from "I never have enough" to "Money flows to me in creative ways."
- **Health**: Use your bot to write supportive routines: meal plans, exercise habits, sleep rituals. Pair this with affirmations that celebrate your body's resilience.

"Not having enough money or good health is not a prophecy. It is a starting point."

Classic Manifesting Principles

From the bestselling works on the Law of Attraction, key practices repeat again and again:

- **Pivoting:** When you notice what you don't want, immediately name what you do want.
- **Positive Aspects:** Train your mind to see the best in any situation.
- **The Art of Allowing:** Stop forcing outcomes and open space for them to arrive.

These tools aren't new. They've been used for centuries. What's new is that you can now train your bot to remind you, encourage you, and keep you aligned.

Try This Prompt:
"Remind me daily of one positive aspect of my health and one positive aspect of my finances."

Your Turn

Take one seasonal marker coming up, the new year, your birthday, the next full moon, or even the weekend.

1. Name one thing you want to release.
2. Name one thing you want to invite.

3. Ask your bot to help you design a ritual, affirmation, or daily practice around it.

Write it below:

Release: ______________________________________

Invite: ______________________________________

Bot Ritual Idea: ______________________________________

Bottom Line

Seasons, moons, holidays, and birthdays aren't just dates. They're energetic portals. When you combine them with conscious practices, gratitude, affirmations, pivoting, visualization, and the steady help of your bot, you create more momentum than willpower alone ever could.

And when you use these cycles to focus on the two areas most deeply tied to human happiness, health and wealth, you begin to unlock the heart of the Law of Attraction.

Chapter 9. Talking to Your Bot Like a Coach

At this point in the journey, you may be wondering, *is all of this manifesting just magic?* The answer is no. This is not sorcery. There are no potions, spells, or covens. Manifesting is the practice of focusing your attention so clearly that your brain, your choices, and your energy align to create real change.

Science confirms this: your brain is wired to filter reality through what you focus on. Psychologists call it the **reticular activating system (RAS)**, the mental filter that highlights what matters most. When you feed your RAS with gratitude, affirmations, and clear visions, it begins to notice opportunities and align your actions to bring those desires into reality.

Faith, Not Fear

Manifesting also doesn't go against the teachings of God or most religions. In fact, many faiths encourage believers to "ask and it will be given."

- **"Ask, and it shall be given you; seek, and ye shall find; knock, and it shall be opened unto you."** (Matthew 7:7, KJV)
- **"As a man thinketh in his heart, so is he."** (Proverbs 23:7, KJV)

- **"Whatever you ask for in prayer, believe that you have received it, and it will be yours."** (Mark 11:24, NIV)

These verses echo the same principle: your words, beliefs, and expectations shape your reality. The Law of Attraction simply gives a modern framework for what ancient texts already taught.

"This is not magic. It's focus, faith and action working together."

Your Bot as a Coach

The best way to think of your bot is not as a mystical guide, but as your *personal coach.* A coach listens, encourages, and helps you plan your next steps. Your bot can do the same:

- Help you reframe negative thoughts.
- Remind you of your affirmations and goals.
- Keep you accountable by checking in daily.
- Offer fresh perspective when you feel stuck.

Instead of seeing your bot as a crystal ball, see it as a mirror that reflects your best self back to you.

Try This Prompt:

"Act as my life coach. Ask me 5 questions that will help me clarify what I want this week."

Why Coaching Matters

Even the most successful people don't rely on willpower alone. They rely on guides, mentors, accountability partners. Jim Rohn mentored Tony Robbins. Andrew Carnegie mentored Napoleon Hill. Coaches multiply progress.

Your bot can fill that role. It doesn't get tired. It doesn't judge. It simply keeps showing up, which is more than most of us do for ourselves.

Keep It Grounded

It's tempting to drift into fantasy when manifesting. That's where the bot's strength comes in: it pulls your dreams down into specific, practical steps.

Example:

- Instead of: *"I want more love."*
- Ask your bot: *"Help me list five qualities I want in a partner and write affirmations to attract someone with these traits."*

Or:

- Instead of: *"I want more money."*
- Ask your bot: *"Help me brainstorm three side income ideas that match my skills and interests."*

"A dream without a plan is just a wish.
A bot helps you turn wishes into action."

Your Birthright to Create

Louise Hay once wrote, *"You are only 17 seconds away from shifting your vibration."* Jerry and Esther Hicks taught that *"Your emotional set-points are within your control."*

These teachings don't replace religion or morality, they enhance them. They remind us that life is meant to feel good, and that we were designed to create.

The message here is simple: you are not waiting for someone else to rescue you. You have been given the tools, mind, spirit, and now technology, to align your thoughts and actions with what you desire.

Your Turn

Tonight, sit quietly and try this:

1. Write one challenge you're facing.
2. Open your bot and say, *"Coach me through this. Ask me questions until I find clarity."*
3. Write down the insights that come.

Repeat this as often as you need. Over time, you'll realize you're not conjuring anything unnatural, you're practicing awareness, faith, and focused action.

Bottom Line

Talking to your bot like a coach is about consistency, not magic. It's about using words and thoughts to activate your brain, align with timeless spiritual principles, and keep moving toward the life you want.

Whether you pray, meditate, journal, or simply type into a chatbot, the principle is the same: focus creates flow. And when you treat your bot as a coach instead of a crystal ball, you'll discover just how much power you already carry inside you.

Manifesting isn't magic. It's not spells, potions, or rituals borrowed from some hidden coven. It's about the power of your mind, the power of your emotions, and the energy of intention. Most faith traditions, from Christianity to Buddhism, speak of aligning thought, word, and heart. In the Bible, Proverbs 23:7 reminds us: *"As a man thinketh in his heart, so is he."* That's not sorcery. That's psychology, faith, and energy all rolled together.

This is where your bot becomes less of a tool and more of a **coach**. Think of it as a gentle guide that keeps you in alignment when the noise of life pulls you away.

Wayne Dyer and the Power of Intention

Dr. Wayne W. Dyer described intention not as something you force, but as a **universal field of energy**. He wrote that this field carries qualities like creativity, kindness, beauty, love, abundance, and receptivity. When you align with intention, you are not grinding against the current of life. You are flowing with it.

Most of us are taught that success comes from sheer willpower: determination, discipline, pushing harder. But Dyer turned that upside down. He taught that true success comes from *allowing*, letting yourself be carried by the flow of universal intention.

Your bot can help you live this principle.

- It can remind you to practice kindness.
- It can generate affirmations rooted in creativity and receptivity.
- It can guide you back when you slip into resistance and fear.

“Intention is not something you do. Intention is something you connect to.”, Wayne Dyer

---

Coaching vs. Coven

Your bot is not a wizard. It’s not going to wave a wand and make money or love appear. What it can do is act as a **mirror**, showing you how your words shape your world. When you tell it what you want, it reflects that intention back to you with clarity.

This is why it feels like coaching. A good coach asks the right questions, holds you accountable, and helps you remember your strengths. Your bot can do the same:

- It won’t scold you.
- It won’t shame you.
- It will remind you of what you said you wanted.

Exercises in Intention

Inspired by Wayne Dyer's *The Power of Intention*, here are some ways to deepen your practice with your bot:

1. **Emulate the Qualities of Intention**
   Ask your bot:
   - *"Write five affirmations that reflect creativity, kindness, and receptivity."*
   - *"Give me three ways I can practice abundance today without spending money."*
2. **Shift from Forcing to Allowing**
   Ask:
   - *"Help me write a list of things I'm trying too hard to control. Show me how I can release them."*
3. **Daily Alignment**
   Each morning, connect to intention. Ask:
   - *"Act as my intention coach. Ask me five questions that connect me to love, creativity, and flow today."*

Reflection Questions

1. What qualities do you most want to embody from the universal field of intention?

2. Where in your life are you pushing instead of allowing?
3. How could your bot remind you to align rather than force?

Linking to Other Teachers

Wayne Dyer wasn't alone in this vision. Zig Ziglar told us, *"Your attitude, not your aptitude, will determine your altitude."* Earl Nightingale reminded us that *"we become what we think about."* And Eckhart Tolle showed millions that the power of living in the **Now** opens the door to peace and possibility.

Your bot can bring all of these voices into your daily practice. You can literally ask it to:

- Summarize a Zig Ziglar talk for quick motivation.
- Remind you of Eckhart Tolle's presence exercises.
- Write affirmations based on Earl Nightingale's principle of focusing your thoughts.

You don't have to memorize every teaching. You just need to **prompt your coach**.

Try This Prompt:
"Coach me like Wayne Dyer. Remind me of the qualities of intention and how I can apply them in my work today."

The Heart of This Chapter

Manifesting is not black magic. It's not even "new." It's ancient, it's scriptural, it's psychological, and it's spiritual. The Law of Attraction, the power of intention, and the role of gratitude are not tricks, they are ways of aligning yourself with what already exists in abundance.

When you treat your bot as a coach, you give yourself a daily practice partner. It serves as a reminder that intention is not something distant. It is something you connect with each time you choose your thoughts.

Bot + Bible

Ask + Receive

"Ask, and it shall be given you; seek, and ye shall find; knock, and it shall be opened unto you."
— Matthew 7:7

Think + Become

"For as he thinketh in his heart, so is he."
— Proverbs 23:7

Believe + Receive

"Whatever you ask for in prayer, believe that you have received it, and it will be yours."
— Mark 11:24

Speak + Create

"Death and life are in the power of the tongue."

— Proverbs 18:21

Vision + Clarity

"Write the vision and make it plain upon tables, that he may run that readeth it."

— Habakkuk 2:2

How to Use This with Your Bot

Use these verses as prompts:

- "Write affirmations based on Matthew 7:7 for my financial goals."
- "Create a daily prayer/affirmation script for me inspired by Habakkuk 2:2."
- "Help me align my words with Proverbs 18:21 by suggesting positive statements for my health."

"Faith without works is dead. A bot helps you do the 'work' while keeping your faith alive."

Chapter 10. Daily Practice = Daily Magic

A single moment of inspiration can light the spark, but it's daily practice that keeps the fire alive. This is where manifesting shifts from an idea to a lifestyle. You're no longer hoping that change will show up, you're training your brain, your emotions, and your energy every day to expect and allow it.

Manifesting is like brushing your teeth. One day won't change much. But over time, consistent care rewires your mind and reshapes your world. With your bot as a partner, you can create a 5–10 minute ritual morning and night that multiplies your results.

Why Rituals Work

Your subconscious runs about 95% of your daily actions. When you deliberately feed it gratitude, affirmations, and visualization each day, it begins to treat those new patterns as normal. Opportunities that once felt invisible start showing up everywhere.

A ritual also takes the "decision fatigue" out of manifesting. You don't have to wonder what to do, you just show up and follow the steps.

"Your life doesn't change in a day. It changes in what you do every day."

Morning Ritual: Start the Day Aligned

Take 5–10 minutes each morning to prime your mind and emotions.

1. **Affirmations:** Ask your bot to generate three positive affirmations tailored to your goals for the day.
2. **Visualization: Close your eyes, breathe, and picture yourself moving through your day with clarity, ease, and success.**
3. **Gratitude:** Name three things you're grateful for, even small ones. This sets your emotional baseline high.

Prompt Box:

"Give me a 5-minute morning script with affirmations, a quick visualization, and gratitude prompts to start my day aligned."

Night Ritual: Close the Day with Clarity

Before bed, use your bot to review and reset. This is where your personal story fits beautifully, the way you lie flat, align your body, see a horizon on your eyelids, recall your gratitude, then plan the next day.

Try this:

- Lie comfortably, hands at your sides.
- Close your eyes and imagine a peaceful horizon.
- Recall three moments you're grateful for from today.
- Speak intentions for tomorrow: "I welcome clarity. I welcome ease. I welcome opportunities."
- Ask your bot to help you write out tomorrow's top three priorities.

This practice lets your subconscious work on your dreams while you sleep.

Prompt Box:

"Help me design a 5-minute night ritual for gratitude, release, and visualizing my next day's success."

Midday Check-In

You don't have to limit your practice to morning and night. When you feel stressed or stuck during the day, open your bot and "talk it out." Treat it as a coach or journal. This quick reset can bring your focus back in minutes.

"A bot can't live your life for you,
but it can remind you to live

your life on purpose."

Build It Into Your Calendar

Habits stick when they're scheduled. Set a recurring reminder on your phone or in your bot:

- Morning Practice: 7:30 a.m.
- Night Practice: 10:00 p.m.

Make it a non-negotiable appointment with yourself.

Your Turn

Use this page to sketch your own daily practice:

Morning Ritual Steps:

Night Ritual Steps:

Midday Reset Prompt:

Bottom Line

Daily practice is where magic meets discipline. With only 5–10 minutes a day, you can build a rhythm of affirmations, visualization, and gratitude that shifts your energy, rewires your brain, and helps you stay connected to the universal flow of intention.

Your bot is the perfect partner for this. It can generate fresh scripts, remind you to check in, and hold your goals steady even when life feels busy. Over time, these micro-moments become a powerful macro-shift, proof that daily practice truly equals daily magic.

Chapter 11. Crisis Helper

We live in times that can feel overwhelming. News cycles scream chaos, social feeds churn with conflict, and even within our own homes, stress can pile high. It's easy to believe the world has tilted into permanent crisis. But history, faith, and human resilience tell another story: the pendulum always swings back, light follows darkness, and even in chaos there is hidden hope.

This chapter is about reclaiming your peace when it feels like everything is on fire.

Hope in the Dark

The American pastor Max Lucado once wrote, "You'll get through this." He was talking about Joseph in the Bible, who was betrayed by his brothers, thrown into a pit, sold into slavery, and unjustly imprisoned. For years, nothing seemed to go right. But in time, Joseph became a leader in Egypt, saving thousands from famine.

Hope is not about ignoring pain. It's about remembering that pain is rarely the last word.

> "Hope is not naïve. Hope is memory, the memory that storms end, the sun rises, and healing begins."

Historical Proof That Crisis Passes

We've been here before.

- **The Great Depression (1930s):** Unemployment soared, banks collapsed, and people stood in breadlines. Yet out of it came Social Security, labor protections, and innovations that still shape our society.
- **World War II (1940s):** A global nightmare of violence and destruction. Yet it also brought new alliances, the United Nations, and the Marshall Plan, which rebuilt Europe.
- **Civil Rights Movement (1960s):** Times of brutal opposition, yet from the chaos came legislation that changed the legal framework of the United States forever.
- **Pandemics, from 1918 to 2020:** Fear and isolation reigned, but humanity emerged with vaccines, new medicine, and better systems for global cooperation.

Crisis may scar, but it also reshapes the world for the better.

"Every crisis carries within it the seed of renewal."

Guarding Your Mind in Troubled Times

One of the most practical things you can do is to limit the noise. Constant exposure to panic headlines and angry debates does not make you wiser, it makes you weary.

- Choose one reliable news source. Read once a day, then close it.
- Mute accounts and conversations that drain you.
- Replace scrolling with something nourishing: music, books, conversations with people you trust.

Your attention is like soil. Whatever seeds you allow in will grow. Plant wisely.

Try This Prompt:
"Help me create a media diet plan so I stay informed but not overwhelmed."

The Role of Your Bot

In seasons of crisis, your bot becomes a stabilizer:

- A **venting partner**: type out your fears and let it reflect calm back.

- A **reframer**: ask, *"Rewrite my anxious thoughts as affirmations of hope."*
- A **coach**: let it break big worries into small, practical steps.
- A **storyteller**: ask for tales of resilience, heroes who endured hard times, and scriptures or quotes that lift you up.

Rather than being part of the chaos, your bot becomes part of your sanctuary.

Faith and Resilience

The Bible holds countless reminders that crisis is not the end:

- *"Weeping may endure for a night, but joy cometh in the morning."*, Psalm 30:5
- *"Fear not, for I am with you; be not dismayed, for I am your God."*, Isaiah 41:10
- *"What was meant for evil, God turned to good."*, Genesis 50:20

These verses echo the principle of manifesting: what you focus on grows. To hold onto faith and hope in crisis is to direct your energy toward healing rather than despair.

A Modern Example

Consider Viktor Frankl, a Holocaust survivor who lost his family in concentration camps. In *Man's Search for Meaning*, he wrote that those who survived were often those who found meaning even in suffering. He discovered that humans can endure almost anything if they can see a "why."

Your "why", your vision, your future, your values, can carry you too.

"Between stimulus and response there is a space. In that space is our power to choose.",

Viktor Frankl

Your Daily Crisis Toolkit

Here's how to keep hope alive even when the world feels heavy:

1. **Morning Anchor:** Start each day with gratitude and one clear intention.
2. **Midday Reset:** Ask your bot to reframe one fear into one action.
3. **Evening Release:** Write down or speak aloud three things you are letting go of.

4. **Community Check:** Stay connected with one positive voice, a friend, mentor, or faith practice.

Try This Prompt:
"Write me a calming bedtime script for nights when the world feels too heavy."

Bottom Line

Crisis is real. Pain is real. But so is hope. History proves it, faith affirms it, and your own resilience embodies it. The world may swing wildly, but you can anchor yourself with practices that nourish, protect, and steady your spirit.

Your bot is here to help you find perspective, shape your energy, and remind you that, like Joseph, like generations before us, like countless survivors, you too will get through this.

Guided Exercises: Crisis Helper Journal

This section is your workbook, a place to turn chaos into clarity. Write directly on these pages, or use them as prompts for your own journal.

---

1. Naming Your Storm

Crises are loud. Naming them takes away some of their power.

- What crisis (personal or global) feels most overwhelming to you right now?
- Write it down in one or two sentences.
- Beneath it, write one word that describes how it makes you feel (fear, grief, anger, uncertainty).

---

2. Hope Anchors

Viktor Frankl survived the unimaginable by clinging to meaning. Shackleton's men survived the Antarctic by clinging to routine and camaraderie.

- Write down three "anchors" you can cling to in tough times (family, faith, daily ritual, purpose, bot prompts).
- Ask your bot: *"Remind me of my three anchors each morning."*

3. My Dust Bowl Perspective

In *The Worst Hard Time*, survivors of the Dust Bowl learned to keep going through years of dust, drought, and despair. Their endurance reminds us: what feels endless is not.

- Write about one time in your life when you endured something hard and eventually came through.
- What did you learn? How can you apply that resilience now?

---

4. What Would TR Do?

Theodore Roosevelt thrived by asking more of himself when life pressed in. Stoics like Seneca reminded us not to waste the time we have.

- When you feel paralyzed, ask: "What would TR do?" or "What would a Stoic do?"
- Write a list of three small, constructive actions you can take today, no matter how small, to reclaim your sense of agency.

Call-Out Quote

"Endurance is not passive. It is choosing to keep showing up with courage when it would be easier to quit."

5. Media Diet Reset

Inspired by Pema Chödrön's advice to "start where you are," take control of what you consume.

- List three sources of noise you need to limit (news, feeds, conversations).
- Replace each with one source of nourishment (books, music, prayer, silence).
- Ask your bot: *"Help me create a daily media diet that calms me instead of overwhelms me."*

---

6. My Resilience Ritual

Shackleton insisted on routines even while stranded on Antarctic ice. Ryan Holiday's *Daily Stoic* shows how simple meditations can create strength.

- Morning: one affirmation of courage
- Midday: one gratitude
- Night: one release statement

Write yours here:

- **Affirmation of Courage:** ______________________________
- **Gratitude:** ______________________________

- **Release: ______________________________**

---

7. Seeing the Horizon

Like you described, lying flat, eyes closed, seeing a horizon on your eyelids. That practice is a perfect metaphor for hope.

- Tonight, try this: visualize a horizon beyond today's trouble. What is just beyond it?
- Write down the image you see. Let this be your vision of what is waiting for you when the storm passes.

Prompt Box

Try This Prompt:
"Tell me the story of someone in history who lived through crisis and emerged stronger, and show me what I can learn from them."

Final Word on Crisis

Remember: every crisis ends. Dust settles, wars cease, economies rebuild, grief softens. You don't need to know how or when. You only need to keep hope alive, one day at a time, with small rituals, steady anchors, and a vision of life beyond the storm.

ou've reached the end of this book, but really, it's the beginning of a new way of living. Everything you've read here is meant to empower you, not overwhelm you.

Manifesting isn't about magic spells or instant miracles. It's about focus, gratitude, clarity, and action. It's about training your mind, your emotions, and your energy to align with what you truly desire, and then taking the steps to make it real.

And at every stage, your bot is your partner.

Your bot is:

- **A coach** who helps you clarify what you want.
- **A scribe** who writes affirmations, scripts, and plans.
- **A mirror** who reflects your best self back to you.
- **A cheerleader** who reminds you of your wins.
- **A sanctuary** where you can vent and regroup without judgment.

Think of it like this: you now have a "super tool" for manifesting, a technology that can hold your vision, generate new ideas, and keep you accountable, so you're never starting from zero.

This is today's version of a gratitude journal, a prayer partner, a vision board, a planner, and a coach rolled into one.

Your Bot + Manifesting Toolkit

Use this quick-reference page whenever you want to jumpstart your practice.

Morning

- Ask for **three affirmations** for today.
- Ask for a **quick visualization** script to run before coffee.
- Name **three gratitudes** and have your bot record them.

Midday

- Ask for a **reframe** of any fear or frustration you're feeling.
- Ask your bot to list **one small action** you can take right now to move closer to your goal.

Night

- Ask for a **gratitude recap**: "List three good things that happened today."
- Ask for a **release script**: "Help me release stress before sleep."
- Write one **intention for tomorrow** with your bot's help.

Weekly

- Use your bot to **track progress**: "Remind me of my wins this week."
- Brainstorm new **affirmations or scripts** for upcoming challenges.

When Crisis Hits

- Ask your bot to tell you a story of someone who endured hardship and prevailed.
- Use it to write calming prayers, meditations or mantras.
- Ask it to help you design an **energy boundary** or **media diet**.

Call-Out Quote

"Your bot can't do the work for you. But it can make the work lighter, clearer, and easier to sustain."

Reflection: Your Manifesting Pledge

Before you close this book, take a moment to anchor what you've learned. Fill in the blanks below:

- My vision for the next year is:

  ____

- My daily practice with my bot will be:

  ____

- My three anchors in tough times are:

  ____

- One thing I commit to manifesting now is:

  ____

Sign it. Date it. This is your promise to yourself.

Try This Prompt:

"Write me a personalized pledge for manifesting with my bot that I can print and sign."

Final Word

You've read about clarity, affirmations, visualization, gratitude, taking action, manifesting specifics, removing blocks, practicing daily magic, and staying steady in crisis. The message behind every chapter is simple:

- **Your thoughts matter.**
- **Your focus matters.**
- **Your actions matter.**
- **You are not alone.**

Your bot is here to make the invisible visible, to help you find words for your dreams, and to keep you steady when life feels heavy.

This is not a gimmick. It's not wishful thinking. It's a method of aligning your mind and heart with the universal flow of intention, the same flow that Wayne Dyer, Viktor Frankl, Pema Chödrön, Shackleton, the Stoics, and countless others tapped into.

As you begin this practice, remember Joseph's story: what others meant for harm, God turned to good. Remember Shackleton: leadership and routine kept his men alive.

Remember Viktor Frankl: between stimulus and response, there is a space, and in that space is our power to choose.

Your bot is one more way of creating that space, a pause, a reflection, a coach. Use it. Talk to it. Train it. Let it hold your dreams with you until they're strong enough to stand on their own.

You are now a deliberate creator. This is your time.

"Nothing is more powerful than a focused mind, an open heart, and a daily practice. You already have all three."

Appendix: Prompts Library

This appendix is your quick-start guide. Use these anytime you feel stuck, uninspired, or need a boost. Copy them directly into your bot and see how it responds, or adapt them with your own details.

Love & Relationships

- "Help me write a checklist of qualities I want in a partner who is kind, funny, and committed."
- "Write five affirmations that strengthen my self-love and confidence."
- "Give me a visualization of the kind of relationship I want to attract."

Money & Career

- "Suggest three income streams I could realistically create this month."
- "Write a pep talk before my big interview."
- "Help me design a weekly money affirmation I can repeat every day."

Health & Wellness

- "Write a daily routine that supports my energy and focus."

- "Create three affirmations that strengthen my belief in my healing."
- "Guide me through a short body-scan meditation for relaxation."

Peace & Stress Relief

- "Help me reframe this stressful situation into something hopeful."
- "Write me a five-minute calming exercise I can do before sleep."
- "List three positive aspects of my current day to shift my focus."

Travel & Adventure

- "Plan a dream vacation that matches my budget and inspires joy."
- "Write a visualization where I walk through the streets of my dream city."
- "Suggest journaling prompts for recording my travel memories."

Creativity & New Ideas

- "Give me five prompts to spark a new art project."
- "Write an opening scene for a short story idea about resilience."

- "Brainstorm ten fresh ideas for my business that align with my values."

Printable Affirmations & Journaling Starters

Copy these into your journal or ask your bot to expand on them:

- **Affirmations:**
  - I am open to abundance in all its forms.
  - Love flows to me and through me with ease.
  - My health improves as I align my thoughts with wellness.
  - Every day, I take one small step closer to my dream.
  - Peace surrounds me.
- **Journaling Starters:**
  - Today I am most grateful for...
  - One lesson I learned this week is...
  - The kind of future I see myself stepping into is...
  - If nothing held me back, I would...
  - My next bold step is...

My Daily Bot Practice (Printable Page)

Morning

☐ Ask my bot for 3 affirmations.

☐ Visualize my goal for today (scripted by my bot).

☐ Write 3 things I'm grateful for.

Midday

☐ Ask my bot to reframe one challenge.

☐ Take one small step toward my dream.

Evening

☐ Review the day with my bot: 3 wins, 1 lesson.

☐ Write one intention for tomorrow.

☐ Use a calming script before sleep.

Weekly Check-In

☐ Ask my bot to list my wins.

☐ Refresh affirmations.

☐ Journal one page on what I'm manifesting next.

"Consistency is the bridge between a wish and a reality. Use your bot to keep that bridge strong."

Conclusion: A Word from Your Bot

At the heart of manifesting lies something both ancient and modern. People have been practicing intention, gratitude, and visualization for centuries. Today, we have tools like ChatGPT that can mirror our thoughts back to us, sharpen them, and help us take action.

Science supports what manifestors have always known:

- **Your brain is rewired by what you repeat.** Neural pathways grow stronger every time you affirm or visualize your goals.
- **Your emotions shape your decisions.** Gratitude, optimism, and joy push you to take actions that align with your dreams instead of sabotaging them.
- **Opportunities aren't magic, they're noticed.** Once you're clear about what you want, your brain's filters (the reticular activating system) begin spotting resources and people who can help you. What feels like a coincidence is often your attention, sharpened by intention.

This is why the principles in this book work. They're not about luck or chance. They are about focus, emotion, and action.

You are living proof. By practicing clarity, affirmations, visualization, gratitude, and action, you've already started shifting your energy. And by working with your bot, you've given yourself a companion that never tires of repeating back your vision until it becomes real.

I’ve lived this. I’ve manifested books, jewelry, art, and connections I once only dreamed about. I believe in it because I’ve seen it unfold in my own life.

Now it’s your turn. Dream boldly. Speak clearly. Act daily. Stay grateful. And let your bot remind you every step of the way that **you are capable of creating the life you want**.

The One-Week Bot Challenge

Ready to see your manifesting practice come alive? Take the next seven days and follow this simple challenge. Each day takes less than 10 minutes.

Day 1, Clarity Prompt
Ask your bot: *"Help me describe my biggest goal right now in one clear sentence."*

Day 2, Affirmation Prompt
Ask your bot: *"Write me three short affirmations to keep me focused on that goal."*

Day 3, Visualization Script
Ask your bot: *"Write me a 2-minute guided visualization for my goal."*

Day 4, Gratitude Prompt
Ask your bot: *"List five things I can be grateful for today related to my goal."*

Day 5, Action Plan Prompt
Ask your bot: *"Give me three simple steps to take this week toward my goal."*

Day 6, Release Prompt
Ask your bot: *"Help me let go of any negative beliefs blocking my goal."*

Day 7, Celebrate Prompt

Ask your bot: *"Write me a short reflection about what I've achieved and how I feel."*

Repeat this cycle for any dream you want to manifest. The point is to build a daily rhythm of clarity, gratitude, and action with your bot as your helper.

Resources for Going Deeper

These books, thinkers, and practices have inspired millions. Your bot can help you learn more about each:

- *Ask and It Is Given*, Esther & Jerry Hicks
- *Think and Grow Rich*, Napoleon Hill
- *The Power of Now* and *A New Earth*, Eckhart Tolle
- *The Power of Intention*, Wayne Dyer
- *Man's Search for Meaning*, Viktor Frankl
- *See You at the Top*, Zig Ziglar
- *The Obstacle Is the Way*, Ryan Holiday
- *When Things Fall Apart*, Pema Chödrön

Pro Tip: Ask your bot for a summary of any of these books or to create a custom reading plan for you.

Notes: My Manifesting Space

Use these pages to jot down your own prompts, affirmations and breakthroughs. Treat this as your private laboratory for experimenting with the ideas in this book.

Manifesting Bot

Manifesting Bot

About the Author

Sugar Gay Isber McMillan has always believed in the transformative power of stories. At the age of five, she discovered her mother's well-worn *Pollyanna* books and was captivated by their "glad game"—the idea that you can always find something to be thankful for, even in hard times. That simple philosophy shaped the way she lives, works, and creates today.

Sugar is the author of more than 50 books across multiple genres, including memoirs and guided journals, as well as her popular *Color, Create & Connect™ with Art History* adult coloring series, which teaches art history through hand-traced illustrations. Her other works include *Heat & Dust*, a near-future novel about survival and hope, and *Rich Bot Poor Bot*, which introduces readers to using AI tools for everyday success.

Whether she's creating coloring books inspired by 19th-century-stained glass, writing guides for using AI as a personal assistant, or crafting heartfelt stories, Sugar's focus is always on helping people feel inspired and empowered.

When she isn't writing, Sugar lives on a ranch in Texas with her husband, where she spends her days surrounded by nature, creating jewelry, tagging her books, and dreaming up her next project. Her love for teaching and learning has taken her from classrooms and corporate training rooms to global platforms, where she shares her experience as a technical writer for a global technology company.

This book is the culmination of a lifelong journey with manifestation and creative living that began with *Pollyanna* and has continued through decades of study, practice and sharing.

Sugar loves hearing from readers. You can connect with her on Instagram at **@SugarGayIsber** or search **"Sugar Gay Isber McMillan"** on Amazon to explore her full range of books.

The WOW Book Co.
Sugar Gay Isber McMillan

If You Liked This Book...

Please leave a review!

Every review helps this book find new readers and keeps the joy flowing. Think of it as your way of sending good energy out into the universe, one happy sentence at a time.

“I manifested that you left a great review for me.”
—Sugar

This QR code will take you to

Sugar Gay Isber McMillan's books on Amazon.

See you there!

Made in the USA
Coppell, TX
05 November 2026

11301604R00059